The Survival Guide for Kids with LD*

*Learning Differences

Revised &
Updated

The Survival Guide for Kids with LD*

*Learning Differences

By Gary Fisher, Ph.D., and Rhoda Cummings, Ed.D.

free spirit
PUBLISHING®

Library of Congress Cataloging-in-Publication Data

Fisher, Gary L.
    The survival guide for kids with LD* : *learning differences / Gary L. Fisher and Rhoda Cummings.—Rev. & updated.
        p. cm.
Summary: Discusses how children with "learning differences" can get along better in school, set goals, and plan for the future.
Includes bibliographical references (   ) and index.
    ISBN 1-57542-119-4
    1. Learning disabled children—Education—United States—Handbooks, manuals, etc.—Juvenile literature. 2. Learning disabilities—United States—Handbooks, manuals, etc.—Juvenile literature. [1. Learning disabilities.] I. Cummings, Rhoda Woods. II. Title.

LC4705.F57 2002
371.9—dc21

2002013289

Reading Level Grade 4; Interest Level Ages 8 & Up;
Fountas & Pinnell Guided Reading Level Q

Edited by Darsi Dreyer
Cover and interior book design by Marieka Heinlen
Illustrated by Jackie Urbanovic

15 14 13 12 11 10 9 8
Printed in the United States of America
W20931210

Free Spirit Publishing Inc.
217 Fifth Avenue North, Suite 200
Minneapolis, MN 55401-1299
(612) 338-2068
help4kids@freespirit.com
www.freespirit.com

For all the kids with LD we've worked with and known,
this book is for you

Contents

Introduction

★ Do you have trouble with schoolwork even though you think you are smart?

★ Do you try to listen to your teacher but you cannot tune out other noises and movement in the room?

★ Do you have a hard time following directions at school?

★ Do you sometimes wake up on school days and wish you could just stay in bed with the covers pulled over your head?

★ Do you wish you had more friends, but you just do not know how to say and do the right things?

★ Do you wish your parents would let you do what you want instead of making you spend hours and hours on homework?

★ Do you feel different—like you do not know where you fit in?

★ Do you feel all alone in the world, as if no one really understands you—including yourself?

If you can say YES to any of these questions, then this book is for you.

This book will answer many questions about LD:

1. Why do kids with LD have trouble learning?

2. What can kids with LD do about having LD?

3. Are kids with LD stupid?

4. Why do kids with LD have a hard time in school?

5. Why don't the other kids understand kids with LD?

This book will not clear up all of your problems. But it can help you understand yourself better. It can give you some ideas about how to make school better for yourself. And it can help you get ready for the future.

After you finish reading *The Survival Guide for Kids with LD*, you might want to write to us. We would be glad to hear from you. Let us know how our book helped you. Or give us some ideas for making our book even better.

You can send a letter to:

Gary Fisher and Rhoda Cummings
c/o Free Spirit Publishing
217 Fifth Avenue North, Suite 200
Minneapolis, MN 55401-1299

Or you can email us at:

help4kids@freespirit.com

Best wishes,

Gary Fisher and Rhoda Cummings

The Six Great Gripes of Kids with LD

Here are the six things that kids with LD say bother them the most:

1. No one explains what LD is, so we spend a lot of time worrying what is wrong with us.

2. We feel confused in school about what we are supposed to do.

3. Our parents, teachers, and the other kids are often not patient with us.

4. We do not have many friends.

5. Kids often tease us and we get in trouble.

6. We do not like being called retarded, stupid, or dumb.

Chapter 1

What Is LD?

People learn in their own ways and at their own speed. Some kids learn to read before they begin school. Others learn to read from their teachers. Some kids may always have a hard time reading. Other kids struggle with spelling or math. Sometimes we say that kids who have trouble learning in school have LD.

What LD Means

When someone has LD, it means that they "learn differently." Other people say LD means a "learning disability." We think "learning differently" better describes kids with LD. Kids with LD are able to learn, but they sometimes need to learn some things in different ways. Everyone learns in their own way.

Not all people with LD are the same. Some have only a few problems learning. Some are great in reading but may have problems learning in another area such as math. Many have problems learning everything from writing to math, reading, and spelling. They might even have trouble learning how to make friends.

A few students have a tough time with all of their schoolwork. But they may quickly learn other things like playing the piano, building a model, or using a computer.

Just because kids with LD have problems learning at school does not mean they are dumb. It means they learn differently from other kids.

This book talks about LD in a way you can understand. It answers questions about school, friends, and the future. But most important, it can help you know that you are not alone.

What LD *Does Not* Mean

It may be hard to know what LD means. But everyone agrees on what LD *does not* mean:

★ It *does not* mean you are dumb.

★ It *does not* mean you are lazy.

★ It *does not* mean you cannot learn.

★ It *does not* mean you will have a low-paying job when you grow up.

You might wish you did not have LD, but do not let LD stop you from becoming the best person you can be.

Kelly* is a very bright kid who has LD. He has trouble with spelling and writing, but he is one of the best math students in his school.

Sherry is eight years old. She has a hard time adding numbers, but she can read very well. Sherry also has LD.

---

*"Kelly" is not the real name of the student. In this book, we do not use the real names of people we know. We use made-up names instead, to respect their privacy.

What Causes LD?

Many scientists think that LD is caused by mixed signals in the brain. When you see, hear, smell, or touch something, your senses send messages to your brain.

The brain is made up of many parts. These parts share information and messages with each other about the rest of the body. Sometimes messages are not sent to the right part of the brain. Sometimes information is messed up while it is traveling to another part of the brain. These mix-ups can make it hard to understand math or reading or spelling or even how to get along with others.

No one knows everything about LD. We do not know why there are so many different ways to have LD. And we do not always know why some people have LD when others do not. There may be many different reasons.

1. Some kids have problems learning from the start. Maybe it is hard for them to learn to catch a ball, or stay in the lines when they color, or understand the rules of a game. Maybe they have trouble learning to talk, or they cannot understand what other people are saying.

When these kids start school, things get worse. All of a sudden they are supposed to read, write, and do math. They try, but they cannot understand how to do these things. They find it very hard to remember numbers and letters. Holding a pencil and writing is difficult, too.

Maybe you remember having some of these problems. Did you feel bad when you could not do as well as the other kids? Were some things hard work for you, when they seemed like fun for other kids?

2. Sometimes LD seems to run in families. If kids have aunts, uncles, or parents with LD, the kids could have LD, too. But there are many people who seem to be the only ones in their families with LD.

3. Some kids with LD had problems when they were babies. Or even before they were born. Maybe their mother was sick. Or maybe they had a hard time being born. Or maybe they got very sick soon after they were born.

Some people think these things could cause LD. But nobody knows for sure.

So, there seem to be many reasons why some people have LD. Until we learn more about LD, this is the best thing we can say about it: *Some kids just have a hard time learning.* And nobody knows exactly why.

How Adults Find Out When a Kid Has LD

Sometimes, students who have a hard time learning get too far behind their classmates. Their teacher asks for help. He or she talks to the LD teacher or the school principal.

Then these kids take some tests (if their parents say it is okay). The tests can help tell if they have LD. If they do, they may start to go to the LD room for some extra help.

It is possible that some of these kids will be able to catch up with their classmates. Then they will no longer go to LD classes. But most kids with LD will always go to LD classes for help. They may always have to learn in a different way, even when they get out of school. Maybe it is because they hear and see things differently from other people.

Are you a kid with LD? Why do you think you have LD? Read on to find out more.

Chapter 2

Why Is It Hard for Kids with LD to Learn?

Do you hear and see things differently from other kids? To find out, ask yourself these questions:

1. When someone tells a joke, do I laugh at the wrong time? Or do I think the joke is not funny?

2. When my teacher gives directions, can I only remember one part of them?

3. When I try to read, do the letters move around on the page?

4. Is it hard to listen to my teacher because I hear other sounds, such as lights buzzing or pencils dropping?

Why is it hard for kids with LD to learn? To help you understand, we will talk about your ears. Then we will talk about your eyes.

How Your Ears Work

Sound travels through the air in sound waves. These waves are like the waves you can see in water. But you cannot see sound waves. You can only hear them.

Your ears are machines that can hear sound waves. The waves go into the ear. The ear has an eardrum and some bones that can change the waves. They change the waves into special signals the brain can understand. Then the sound can travel to the brain and the brain can identify the sound.

Let's say a dog barks. The sound of the bark travels to your ears in sound waves. The sound waves move through the ear and into the brain. The brain tells you that the sound is a bark.

For some kids with LD, the brain cannot understand what the ears send it. A dog barks, and the sound waves reach the ear. But the signal gets mixed up and the brain "hears" something else. Or maybe the brain cannot tell that the sound came from the dog.

Read what R.J. says about having LD:

"I can't hear good. I can't talk good. I can't write good. Sometimes it's hard to figure out the right answer. It's hard to learn." —R.J., 11

How Your Eyes Work

Your eyes take in whatever you look at. Like your ears, they have a special way of sending what they take in to the brain. It is the brain's job to help you understand what you are seeing.

Let's say you are looking at the word READ. Your eyes see the letters R E A D. If you have good eyes, you can see the letters clearly. Your eyes send the four letters to your brain. Then your brain must decide that those four letters are the word READ. You might start to think about a kid reading a book.

For some kids with LD, the eyes may see the word READ. But the signal "READ" never gets to the brain. The brain thinks it sees something else instead. Maybe the letters are moving all over the paper. Or the letters are blurred together in a funny way.

Do you have trouble reading? Maybe it is because the signals in your brain cannot give you the right words. Your eyes are okay. They work like everyone else's eyes do. But your brain "sees" the words differently.

Ways to Learn—Even if Your Brain Works Differently

Other problems may happen when a brain works differently.

Some kids with LD have no sense of time. Others do not have good body balance. Some cannot understand what other people want or are feeling. Still others seem to see and hear everything that is going on at once. It is hard for them to pay attention to one thing at a time.

How can you learn if your brain works differently? LD teachers have ways to help. If reading is hard for you, perhaps you can listen to books on tape. If you can read, but you cannot understand what your teacher or parents tell you, then maybe they can write things down for you instead. If you have a hard time spelling, maybe you can use a spellchecker on a computer. If you have problems with simple math, maybe you can use a calculator. There are lots of different ways to learn!

If you do not understand what you see or hear, tell your teachers. Ask them to help you think of other ways to learn. Then you can learn things the other kids do. You will just learn them in your own way.

Other Ways to Learn

Here are some ideas for other ways to learn. Your teacher can help you think of more.

★ Ask a friend or a teacher for help.

★ Trace new words with your fingers as you read them.

★ Use a bookmark or another piece of paper to help you follow the text and keep your place as you read.

★ Read aloud instead of reading silently.

★ Build a model or draw a picture instead of writing a report (but first, ask your teacher if this is okay).

★ Ask your teacher if you can put fewer math problems on a page.

★ Write math problems on graph paper to line the numbers up straight. Or turn your lined paper sideways to help you separate the numbers.

★ Learn to use a computer for writing. Or ask your teacher if you can use printing rather than cursive writing.

★ Ask your teacher if you can have an extra set of textbooks to keep at home.

★ Ask if you can use your teacher's notes to help you study for tests.

★ Ask your teacher if you can have extra time when taking tests.

Remember: If You Need Help, Ask!

Ask your teachers. Ask your parents. Do not keep it a secret.

Pages 84–96 list several resources that can help you learn. Show these pages to your parents and teachers.

Chapter 3

Seven Kinds of LD

Now you know some things about why people have LD. And you know some things about why it is hard for kids with LD to learn.

But did you know that there are many different kinds of LD? Reading about these will help you understand more about LD.

1. Talking and Listening LD (Speech and Language LD)

Kids with talking and listening LD have good ideas, but they cannot find the right words to tell other people about their ideas. They might talk slowly or struggle with their words. They might not make the right sounds with their mouths.

They hear when other people talk, but they have a hard time understanding what the words mean. People sometimes think they do not listen.

Kids with this kind of LD might ask other people to say things over again. Sometimes those people get angry or laugh at them.

Shawn had talking and listening LD. One day his history teacher was telling the class about the different kinds of Indian arrowhead points. When she asked the class to name the different kinds of points, Shawn raised his hand. He said, "The first one is the decimal point." All the kids in the class laughed. Shawn laughed, too, but he did not know what he had said that was so funny.

2. Reading LD

Some kids have trouble reading. Reading is much harder for them than it is for other kids. They might have trouble learning the alphabet or sounding out words. They might not be able to hear rhymes like "cat" and "hat."

Sometimes the letters and words seem to move on the page. Kids with reading LD might skip lines when they read or read some lines more than once. They have a hard time understanding what they read.

Aleisha says it was hard for her to read. For her, it seemed like the letters kept moving up off the paper. She works with an LD teacher several times a week to help her read better. She also brings a tape recorder to class so she can tape things she needs to remember.

3. Writing LD

Some kids have a tough time with writing. They have many ideas in their heads and can talk about them, but they have trouble putting them down on paper. Writing with good grammar is challenging for them, and so is spelling because they mix up the letters of the alphabet. Their handwriting is hard to read. Their school papers might be very messy. Sometimes they get low grades because of this.

Jermaine has LD. His writing is hard to read and it takes him a long time to put his thoughts on paper. He learned to write using a computer. He is very excited because he had always gotten low grades for messy papers. His papers often had holes in them because he had to erase so much. Now he can fix his mistakes on the computer, and he can turn in neat, clean papers.

4. Math LD

Many kids with math LD have trouble with numbers. Math problems are difficult for them. They do not understand what the numbers or symbols mean. They might have trouble memorizing math facts or lining up numbers. Even if they memorize how to do something in math, they do not understand what the answer means.

Shayla has math LD. She has trouble remembering her math facts. She gets special help in math. Her teacher lets her use a calculator to add and subtract. That way she can continue to learn about fractions and the number line.

5. Organizing Skills LD

Some kids with LD have trouble getting organized at all. They forget their assignments. They leave their homework on the school bus. If someone gives them too many directions at one time, they forget what they need to do. Their desks at school or rooms at home may look like they were hit by a tornado. Some kids have a hard time keeping track of time and are always late for class or activities. This can upset people who are waiting for them.

Pablo usually knew how to do his homework. He would start it but sometimes forget to finish it. He got poor grades at school because he did not turn in all of his papers. His teacher had a meeting with Pablo and his parents. Together they came up with a way he could keep track of his assignments. His teacher now gives him a written homework sheet. His parents sign the sheet after Pablo finishes his homework.

6. Social Skills LD (Nonverbal LD)

Sometimes kids with LD read, write, and do math well. They might also be very organized. But they have trouble "reading" people. They laugh or speak at the wrong time and interrupt conversations. They do not get jokes that their friends tell. They stand too close to the person they are talking to.

People often show what they are thinking and how they feel by what they do. They send "signals" with their bodies, voices, and words. To most people, a frown is a signal that someone is unhappy. An angry voice means "Watch out!"

Kids with this kind of LD cannot understand these "signals." They cannot tell how other people are feeling. They might have trouble making friends.

Ray has LD and has a hard time making friends. He often interrupts when other people are talking. His classmates sometimes call him pushy. Ray works with an LD teacher who is helping him to "read" other people's body signals, and now he does not interrupt as much. He gets along a lot better with his classmates.

7. Motor LD

Kids with motor LD have a hard time controlling their muscles. They move slowly. They might have trouble running, riding a bike, jumping, hopping, and playing sports. They lose their balance easily. They are teased for being clumsy.

Some have trouble using their hands and fingers. It is difficult for them to hold a pencil or to use scissors. Their handwriting is hard to read. They have trouble buttoning their shirt, tying their shoes, or using forks and spoons during meals.

Felicia has a hard time in gym class. She cannot run very well and she has trouble throwing and catching. She goes to Adaptive P.E., which is a special gym class for kids who need extra help learning basic movement skills.

What kind of LD do you think you have? Do you have more than one kind of LD?

Chapter 4

A Law to Help LD Kids Learn

Many years ago, no one ever said, "That person has LD." But even then, some smart kids had trouble learning. But they did not always get the help they needed at school. Their parents wanted to help them. They knew their children were smart and could learn. They wanted teachers and other people to think of ways to help their children.

All over the country, parents began to talk to teachers and school principals. They began to work together. Parents of kids with LD worked with other parents whose kids had LD to make sure their kids could learn. They wanted schools to teach ALL kids— those with LD and also those with other problems.

In 1975, congress passed a law called IDEA.* This law is important for many reasons.

★ The law says that all kids, no matter what kind of problems they have, must be allowed to go to school.

★ It says that all kids must be taught in the ways and classes that help them learn.

---

*The law was originally called Public Law 94-142 "The Education for All Handicapped Children Act of 1975." It was revised and changed to IDEA (Individuals with Disabilities Education Act) in 1990.

★ It also says that no students will be put into a special class just because they score low on one test. Or because they speak a different language. Or because of their race or family background.

The law has been updated many times since 1975. It still protects the rights of kids with LD. The law describes how schools must identify kids who have LD and plan to help them learn.

What the Law Means for Students with LD

The law means that kids with LD have a right to get the help they need. It says that students with LD should learn in the classroom that is best for them.

Many kids with LD learn in regular classrooms. They leave their regular classrooms to go to a place called the "resource room." The resource room teacher helps them with the work they do in the regular classroom.

Resource room (RĒ sors rōōm)

means "a room where students with special needs go for part of the day to get special help with their schoolwork."

Other kids with LD learn better in small classrooms. They need to have special ways to learn reading, math, and writing all day long.

Tran is 10 years old. He goes to a resource room for one hour a day. He has a lot of friends who do not have LD. He has some trouble with reading, but he is good at math, and he likes to play soccer. His resource room teacher helps him with his reading.

Kendra is the same age as Tran. When she talks, it is hard to understand her. She has trouble with all of her schoolwork. When she was in a regular classroom, the kids sometimes teased her. They said things like, "You talk funny!"

Because she needs more help in school than Tran does, Kendra goes to a special classroom all day long. She gets special help with all her schoolwork. With good help, maybe someday she will go to some classes in a regular classroom.

LD teachers do more than just help kids with schoolwork. LD teachers help students listen and talk better, write better, even make friends easier. As kids with LD learn to do these things, they can start spending less time with an LD teacher and more time in a regular classroom.

For many kids with LD, the LD room is a place where it is quieter and easier to pay attention. It is a place where it is always okay to have learning differences.

People with LD *can* learn many things, even if they must learn them in different ways. Some people with LD are very smart—even gifted!

This does not mean that school will be easy for you. It means that you *can* learn. How easy or how hard it will be depends on YOU yourself, and on your parents and teachers.

The good news is this: You are as smart as the other kids! You can learn what they can learn!

The trick is to know this: You learn *differently.* Ask for help to find a different way. Then you can learn!

Chapter 5

Getting into an LD Program

IDEA says that *all* kids, no matter what kind of problems they have, must be allowed to go to school. It says that *all* kids must be taught in the right kind of classes to help them learn.

This means kids with LD, as well as kids with other special needs, too.

Other Kinds of Kids with Special Needs

In addition to LD kids, other kids with special needs get extra help or go to special classes at school.

1. Mentally impaired means "slow to learn and not able to learn many things." These kids have "developmental disabilities." This means they have a hard time learning and they fall behind their peers in school. They also have trouble learning how to care for themselves. Some things they will never be able to learn. Many of these kids are in a special classroom for the whole day and not in a regular classroom.

2. Speech or language disability means having a hard time talking or understanding what other people are saying. Sometimes kids with this disability stutter or mix up sounds. It is hard for others to understand what they are saying. They are usually in a regular classroom but will leave to meet with a speech therapist.

3. Hearing or vision impairment means having trouble hearing or seeing. Depending on how well they can hear or see, sometimes they are in the regular classroom. Some kids are not able to hear or see at all. Sometimes they go to a special school.

4. Emotional or behavioral disorder means having problems with the way one acts or feels. These kids act out and are often in trouble. They are sometimes mean and bossy to other kids and adults. They can get angry very easily.

How the Law Works

LD classes are separate from other special needs classes. The law tells your school how to decide who has LD and who can be in LD classes. For each student with LD, it may happen a little differently.

When **Reggie** was nine years old, his mom took him to the doctor because he was having stomachaches. The doctor could not find anything wrong with Reggie. So she talked with him. She asked Reggie if anything was wrong at school or home.

When Reggie said he did not like school, the doctor asked him some questions about schoolwork. She talked to Reggie's mom about what Reggie was like when he was younger.

The doctor thought Reggie might have LD. So she had his mom ask to have him tested for LD at school. Reggie was tested. The tests showed that he had LD. After Reggie began to get help from the LD teacher, his stomach-aches went away.

When Sheila was 10 years old, her dad read a story in a magazine about LD. He thought Sheila sounded like the kids in the story. He called Sheila's teacher to ask how he could find out if Sheila had LD. The teacher thought that Sheila was just slow to learn. But the teacher made sure Sheila got tested. It turned out that Sheila did have LD. So she got the reading help she needed in the resource room.

How Did You Get into an LD Program?

You read Reggie's story and Sheila's story. Different kids get into LD programs in different ways and for different reasons.

How did *you* get into an LD program? Maybe your story goes something like this.

First your teacher or your parents may have noticed that you were having a problem with learning. Your teacher and your mom or dad talked to each other. Your teacher asked if some other people at your school could meet you and try to help.

If your parents agreed, then you probably were given some tests. Do you remember these tests? Perhaps you made shapes with blocks or copied shapes from cards. Maybe you repeated numbers or words. Maybe you put pictures in order to tell a story.

You also took tests in reading, spelling, and math. Maybe you listened to a story and then answered some questions about the story. Maybe you were asked to tell what certain words mean. You might have listened to sounds and tried to figure out what words they made.

Another person probably tested your ears to check your hearing, and your eyes to check your sight. Someone may have come into your class to watch you for a while to see how you follow directions, pay attention, and do your work. You may not have known that person was even there.

Your teacher and your parents also may have described where they thought you had trouble learning. They may have said how they think you learn best.

After these things were done, your teacher, the people who tested you, and your mom or dad got together to decide if you needed help because of LD.

If your teacher and the people who tested you thought you should have some special help, they met with your parents in an IEP meeting. At this meeting, everyone decided what you should learn and how you would be taught. Together they came up with a special plan that was just right for you.

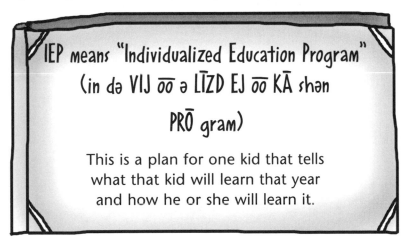

IEP means "Individualized Education Program"
(in də VIJ oo ə LĪZD EJ oo KĀ shən PRŌ gram)

This is a plan for one kid that tells
what that kid will learn that year
and how he or she will learn it.

Your parents and teachers will discuss your IEP each year. The plan can then be updated to fit where you are in your learning. The law says that students with LD must be tested again every three years. This is to see if they still need help because of LD.

Maybe you did not think you were lucky when you found out you had LD. But many kids have problems with learning and never know why. They never get the help they need to succeed. So, in a way, you *are* lucky. You can get the right kind of help, so you can learn as much as possible.

"The LD room gives me more help than the other class. That's why I go. The other kids don't mess with me when I go." —Joe, 10

Kids with LD Are Smart

Maybe other kids call you names because you go to an LD class or maybe they tease you because you get extra time in class to do your work. Some kids are just plain mean. They want to make you feel bad. They will tease anybody they can.

Teasing from other kids may remind you that you have trouble with learning. Perhaps sometimes you even wonder if you are just stupid.

How Smart Are You?

If you wonder about this, here are some things to keep in mind: You must be as smart as most other kids in order to be in an LD class. Some kids with LD are even smarter than most other kids. They may go to both LD and gifted classes.

Howard Gardner, a professor at the Harvard School of Education, has found eight different ways that people are smart. He calls these eight ways *multiple intelligences*. Everyone is smart in all eight ways. Some kids may be smarter in some areas than in others, but everyone is smart in his or her own way. Here are the eight ways you can be smart.

1. Word smart means that you are good at writing, reading, spelling, and talking. You have an easy time using words.

2. Number smart means that you are good at math and using numbers. You are also good at riddles and computers.

3. Picture smart means that you are good with images and have an eye for detail. You can paint, draw, build, and design things.

4. Music smart means that you are good at patterns, tempos, rhythms, and sounds. You are probably good at singing or playing a musical instrument.

5. Body smart means that you are good at moving your body. You might be good at sports or dancing. You might also be good at crafts like sewing, carving, or building models.

6. People smart means that you are good at understanding other people and their feelings. You might be a good leader.

7. Self smart means that you understand yourself very well. You are aware of your own feelings, ideas, and dreams.

8. Nature smart means that you enjoy the outdoors and have a connection with plants, animals, and your surroundings. You might be good at gardening or cooking.

As you can see, just because you might have trouble reading or doing math problems does not mean that you are not smart. It just means that you might be more body smart or people smart than you are word smart or math smart. There are plenty of ways that you can be smart.

How Much Can You Learn?

If you are a kid with LD, you probably have "learning ups and downs."

Some days it is hard to learn something new, like how to multiply numbers. You might try and try, but you still have trouble catching on. Then one day, all of a sudden, you understand! You do ten math problems and YOU GET THEM ALL RIGHT!

Kids with LD may learn some school subjects slowly. They might need the help of extra time for tests or a calculator for math. They may learn other things just as well as, or even better than, other kids.

Most kids with LD spend most of their time in a regular classroom. They learn the same things the other kids learn. They just go to the LD room or the resource room for extra help. Or they have other things that help them learn in class.

How Will You Do When You Get Out of School?

Most kids with LD have a hard time in school. But with good help, most of them go on to become successful adults. Some kids with LD go to college. Others find jobs they enjoy. They may fall in love, have good friends, find hobbies. In other words, most kids with LD grow up to be independent.

Independent (in di PEN dənt)

means "able to live on one's own and take care of oneself."

People with LD Who Did Not Give Up

Nelson Rockefeller
He became Vice President of the United States and governor of New York. He had a severe reading problem.

Tom Cruise
This movie actor has a reading disability.

Ann Bancroft
She was held back in school because she had trouble learning how to read. She is an arctic explorer, and she was the first woman to reach the North Pole.

Woodrow Wilson
He became President of the United States. He did not learn to read until he was 11 years old.

Erin Brockovich
This legal assistant has dyslexia, but she did not let that stop her from helping bring to trial a case against a company that was polluting the groundwater in California.

Whoopi Goldberg
She has succeeded as an actress and comic, despite having reading problems in school.

Chapter 7

How to Deal with Sad, Hurt, Angry Feelings

Darnell was in third grade. He was a quiet kid who liked animals and art and kickball. But one day, Darnell surprised his dad by saying that he did not want to go to school anymore. He missed the school bus on purpose, and his dad had to drive him to school.

The next day and the next were the same. Darnell couldn't tell his dad *why* he did not want to go to school. He just did not want to be there. His teacher said that nothing unusual had happened. He had many friends and was doing okay in school. He was having some problems with spelling and writing, but his teacher was not worried.

His dad talked to other teachers who knew Darnell. One said that maybe they should test Darnell for LD. His dad thought that might be a good idea.

The tests showed that Darnell had writing LD. He cried when the psychologist and his dad talked to him about it. He did not want anyone to know how hard writing was for him.

But with special help in school, his writing improved. Having a chance to talk about his problems with people who understood helped Darnell feel better. He did not like having LD, but now he knew how to get the help he needed. He started to feel better about school again.

Why Kids with LD Have These Feelings

Many kids with LD become unhappy. They do not think they are learning fast enough. Some of them have trouble getting along at school. Or they have trouble sitting still. Other kids laugh at the things they do and say. Then the kids with LD feel sad, hurt, and angry.

Read what these kids say:

"I don't like being LD. It makes me mad. I don't like how I talk." —John, 11

"Kids laugh at me because I can't add numbers. I cry every day at school." —Rona, 10

"Kids are mean to me. They call me names like stupid. My brothers tease me all the time because of the way I talk. I get mad because I have a problem. I don't like it. I wish I was like other kids." —R.J., 11

When kids feel sad, hurt, and angry, they sometimes say they do not want to go to school. Or they might make themselves sick. Some kids get mad at their parents, teachers, brothers, sisters, or other kids. Others get into trouble or stop trying to do their schoolwork.

Sometimes it seems that no one understands or cares what is happening. Other kids, teachers, or parents do not understand.

Often, kids with LD do not know why they feel sad, hurt, and angry. The teacher or parent says, "Why did you throw that book?" The kid with LD says, "I don't know." He or she is telling the truth. It is hard for kids to explain why they feel the way they do.

When kids cannot tell someone about their sad, hurt, and angry feelings, the feelings do not go away. (This is true for everyone, not just kids.) So the kids just keep feeling sad, hurt, and angry. It is hard for them to have fun. It is hard for them to do their schoolwork. It is hard for them to think about anything besides their feelings. We call this feeling depressed.

Depressed (di PREST)

means "feeling sad all the time."

Six Ways to Help Yourself Feel Better

Do you ever feel depressed? Here are six things you can do to help yourself feel better.

1. Do some "I like me" exercises. If you exercise your arms, your arm muscles will get bigger. If you exercise the "I like me" part of your brain, it will get stronger.

Here are some "I like me" exercises you can try.

In the morning:

★ Look in the mirror and think of five things you like about yourself. Say each thing out loud: "I like my _____."

★ Find five ways you would like to do better. Say them out loud, too.

At night:

⭐ Look in the mirror and tell yourself how well you did that day. Say: "Today I did better at _____."

Do these exercises each morning and each night until you feel better. If you like them, keep doing them.

2. Draw your feelings. If you have trouble talking about how you feel, try drawing pictures that show how you feel. For many kids with LD, this is easier than talking. You can show your pictures to a parent or another adult you trust.

3. Have a chat with a counselor.

Counselor (KOUN səl ər)

means "someone who helps people by listening and giving advice."

Many schools have counselors who are trained to help kids who feel depressed. Other counselors may work in offices near where you live.

You can tell your parents that you want to talk to a counselor. Your teacher or principal may be able to give you some names of counselors. Or your doctor can help you find a counselor.

Even if you are not sure what to say, counselors can often help you talk. You may need to see a counselor a number of times before you start to feel better.

4. Make a book about yourself. You can write a book about yourself. Or you can draw a book. Or you can make a book with both words and pictures.

Your book can have these parts:

Chapter 1: Things I Like Best About Myself

Chapter 2: Things I Would Like to Change
            About Myself

Chapter 3: Things That Make Me Feel Happy

Chapter 4: Things That Make Me Feel Sad, Hurt,
            or Angry

Chapter 5: How I Want to Be in 10 Years

5. Take life one day at a time. Do you sometimes think that you will NEVER get out of school? Do you worry about high school? Do you wonder if you will ever be independent?

Worrying does not help. Try not to worry about the future. Instead, promise yourself every morning that you will do your best TODAY.

6. Be patient. When you are upset and want to give up, think about this: Many people with LD did not give up. (Remember the list of people who didn't give up on page 35?)

Remember that you will not be in school forever. Remember that most of your teachers care about you and want you to learn. Most parents love their kids and want to help, too.

But most of all, remember that you are special. No one else is like you. Look inside and see all the good things. Do not take yourself too seriously. Learn to laugh at yourself. Be patient!

On pages 89–90 of this book, there is a part called "A Few Words About Depression." Show this part to your parents and teachers.

Chapter 8

Ten Ways to Get Along Better in School

A lot of kids with LD do not like school. After all, it is not fun to have problems learning, especially when most of the other kids are not having problems. That may be why so many kids with LD get into trouble at school.

Read what these kids say about school:

> "Well, one thing I know is you shouldn't daydream. When you daydream, it's kind of like being in love. You just sit there. If you do that, you won't learn too much." —LeDale, 9

> "Sometimes I try to be real funny in class, but the teacher still frowns." —Damien, 9

"When I'm in trouble, I sit in a corner and read my palms." —Rob, 10

"My teacher says I bother other kids. I'd rather talk than struggle with fractions."
—Brianna, 11

There are some kids with LD who *do* like school. Maybe they do not like it all of the time, but they like it some of the time.

Read what these kids say about school:

"The principal helps me with problems. My teacher reads with me and talks to me."
—Chris, 11

"I always go to the counselor so I can get out of class, but then she helps me." —Gabriel, 12

"I love art class. I do really good in art. Reading is hard but art is fun." —Sindi, 10

If you do not like school, you can do something about it. There are ways to get along better in school. Here are 10 ways for you to try.

1. When things are tough, have a chat.

Often, kids with LD do not share their feelings with others. They feel sad, hurt, and angry, but they keep these feelings bottled up inside of them.

It is hard to keep feelings bottled up. Sooner or later, the feelings will come out. Sometimes they come out in strange ways. Some students with LD stop doing their schoolwork. Or they throw things, get into fights, or talk back to teachers. They get into trouble, and they feel even worse.

When you are feeling sad, hurt, and angry, why not find someone to talk to? How about a school counselor, a teacher, a janitor, an aide, a bus driver, or a friend? Pick someone you like and trust, someone who will understand. Then go talk to that person.

2. Keep your head up!

Having LD is nothing to be ashamed of. If someone asks you why you go to LD classes or why you get extra time to finish a test, tell them (if you feel like it). Look them in the eye and say, "I have LD." Or say, "I learn differently from other kids. The LD classes help me learn."

Believe and act like you are important. The more you do this, the more other people will treat you like an important person.

3. Become an expert.

An expert is someone who is the best at something. Kids with LD can become experts, just like anyone else can.

Think of things that kids your age are interested in. What about collecting baseball cards? Listening to rock music? Braiding hair? Pick something you like that other students in your class like, too. Then find out as much as you can about it. Ask your teacher and your parents to help you.

This is a good way to show that kids with LD can be smart. It is also a good way to get attention. When you are an expert, other people will ask you for help.

4. Take part in school activities.

School is more fun when you do things other than just schoolwork. Take part in school activities like plays, clubs, or sports. Offer to help plan school activities. Let your teachers know that you want to help.

5. Learn more about LD.

Find out as much as you can about your kind of LD and the ways you learn. When you have teachers who do not understand LD, you can tell them about it. This will help them plan for you.

On pages 74–82 of this book is a part called, "Ten More Things You Might Want to Know About LD." Read this part. Show it to your parents and teachers.

6. Make friends.

Some kids with LD make friends only with each other. It is good to have friends with LD. But it is better to have friends who have LD *and* friends who do not.

In Chapter 10 of this book, we will tell you some ways to make both kinds of friends. If you want to read these now, turn to pages 58–61.

7. Be a helper.

Many kids with LD feel like they are always asking for help. They feel like they are the only ones who ask for help.

But you can be a helper, too! Maybe you can help younger kids who are learning things you already know. Or you can help another student in your class with something you do well. If you know you can help, tell someone! Offer to help.

8. Stay out of trouble.

For many kids with LD, schoolwork is hard and boring. So they join in when other kids start fooling around. (After all, fooling around is more fun than working!)

This kind of joining in is not a good idea. It gets teachers and parents upset. If you see other kids fooling around, just ignore them. Keep doing your schoolwork. Then you will stay out of trouble.

9. Know how to relax and cool off.

Think of the last time you were working on something very hard that you did not understand. Maybe you got upset and angry.

What did you do next? Did you pretend to keep working when you were really not working? Did you yell? Throw your work on the floor? Quit? Cry? Go home?

These things will not help you get along better in school. You need to come up with other things to do instead.

Maybe you can raise your hand and ask your teacher for help. But what if your teacher is busy? Then you need to help yourself.

Here are ways you can help yourself:

★ Close your eyes, take three deep breaths, and count to 10 very slowly and quietly.

★ Say "relax" to yourself five times very slowly and quietly.

When you start to feel better, try doing your work again.

10. Do not use LD as an excuse!

Some kids use LD as an excuse for not doing their schoolwork.

Maybe a kid has science homework to do. But there is a movie on TV he wants to watch. So he watches the movie instead. The next day, he tells his teacher, "I forgot to do my homework because I have LD."

Or maybe another kid has a math lesson to do. But she does not want to do the lesson. So she tells her teacher, "I am no good at math because I have LD."

Or another kid has a spelling test coming up. He does not want to study for the test. He wants to play outside instead. So he tells his teacher, "Spelling tests upset me because I have LD."

NEVER use LD as an excuse for not doing your work! It is your teacher's job to find the best ways to teach you. It is your job to work as hard as you can.

Even with the best teachers and the best books, some things will be hard for you. But NEVER use LD as an excuse for not trying.

Chapter 9

What to Do When Other Kids Tease You

It is not right, but kids tease each other all the time. They tease anyone who dresses, talks, looks, or acts differently from them. Probably everyone gets teased at some time.

Why Kids Tease

There seem to be three main reasons why kids tease. Here are the reasons:

1. They see other kids doing it, and they want to be a part of the group.

2. They have been teased, and they are trying to hurt someone else the way they were hurt.

3. They think that if they make someone else feel bad, they will feel better. (This does not work!)

Have you ever teased anyone? What did you tease them about? Have you ever been teased? How did it make you feel? Which do you remember most: teasing other kids or being teased?

Why You Get Teased

Because you have LD, you are different from other kids. Remember that kids tease anyone who dresses, talks, looks, or acts differently from them. Because you are different, kids probably tease you. Maybe you even get teased a lot.

★ Maybe you get teased about going to LD classes. ("There's the kid in the dummy class!")

★ Maybe kids call you names. ("Stupid!" "Retard!")

★ Maybe some kids let you know that they do harder schoolwork than you do. ("You are only reading Book Two? I finished that book last year.")

★ Maybe you get teased about the kind of schoolwork you do. ("That is baby work!" "You are the worst reader in our class!")

No matter how other kids tease you, you probably feel sad, hurt, and angry. Being teased is no fun.

The good news is, you *can* do something about teasing. There are ways you can act and things you can say when other kids tease you. Some of these are not so helpful. Some are kind of helpful. And some are very helpful. When you read about them, ask yourself, "Which ones do I do?"

Think about this:

You cannot control the kids who tease you, but you can control what you do when they tease you.

Not So Helpful Things to Do When You Get Teased

What You Can Do	What Might Happen
Start a fight.	You might get beat up.
	If you win the fight, you might feel better for a while. You could also get into trouble for fighting.
	If you win the fight, that kid might stop teasing you. But then someone else, maybe bigger and stronger, could start teasing you.
Tease back.	The kid teasing you might be a lot better at it than you are. Then you will feel even worse.
	The kid might tease you again because you teased back the first time.

Not So Helpful Things to Do When You Get Teased
(continued)

What You Can Do	What Might Happen
Cry and run away.	Now the kid knows that teasing really bothers you. He or she might keep it up. You might feel bad about not standing up for yourself.

Kind of Helpful Things to Do When You Get Teased

What You Can Do	What Might Happen
Ignore the teasing.	Soon the teasing may stop. However, some kids can keep it up for a long time. They may try harder if they see you are trying to ignore them.
Smile and say it does not bother you.	This is a lot like ignoring. It is hard to do. It is also not good to hide your feelings.

Very Helpful Things to Do When You Get Teased

What You Can Do	What Might Happen
Stand up straight and look the kid in the eye. Say in a calm voice, "I do not like to be talked to that way." Then walk away.	Even if the teasing does not stop, you will feel good about standing up for yourself. And you will not get in trouble for fighting. The kid teasing you may see that he or she cannot make you cry and get angry. The kid may give up trying. You may have to repeat this many times before the kid "gets it." But that is still better than fighting or hiding your feelings.
Talk to an adult you like and trust. Pick a person who is a good listener and who cares about you. Tell that person about the teasing and how you feel.	You will feel better! No one can make kids stop teasing. But you can talk about your feelings, and that always helps.
Do not tease others.	You are a lot less likely to be teased if you do not tease.

Remember:

You cannot control the kids who tease you. But you can control what you do when they tease you.

Read what these kids say about being teased:

"When all my crayons got stolen, I just went to the kid and got them back!" —Rex, 8

"If the kids on the playground keep on following me, I just tell the teacher or ignore them." —Stacy, 11

"When other kids make fun of me, I want to slug them, but I try to ignore them."
—Reiko, 11

"I talk to my teacher when kids make me mad. She helps me figure out what some of the kids really said." —Marcus, 11

Chapter 10

Tips for Making and Keeping Friends

Having friends makes school more fun. But it is not always easy to make friends. Going to LD classes can make it even harder. But this does not mean you cannot do it! Kids with LD can have friends, just like everyone else.

Kenny was nine when he found out he had LD. He already had a lot of friends in his regular classroom. He was a friendly boy who helped others and did not tease others. At first he did not want to go to the resource room for help. But his mom and dad said he had to go.

When Kenny started going to the resource room, he made new friends. But he also kept his old friends. He stayed in LD classes all through grade school and high school. And he always had a lot of friends. Kenny had a talent for making and keeping friends.

The "Making Friends Rules"

Kenny also knew about the "making friends rules." These are different from other kinds of rules.

You do not find them written down in books. You do not find them on signs. You learn them from other people. You learn them from things that happen in your life. Some of them you learn by making mistakes.

Read what these kids say about the "making friends rules":

> "I learned the hard way not to push kids down at the bus stop. I got pushed down myself." —Karla, 9

> "Just because you feel bad you don't have to make someone else feel bad, too." —José, 10

> "You should be nice and gentle with other people's belongings." —Amani, 8

Some kids with LD have trouble learning the "making friends rules," just like they have trouble learning to read, spell, or do math.

Ways to Make All Kinds of Friends

Think about the friends you have. Are they all kids who go to LD classes? It is good to have friends who have LD. But it is better to have friends who have LD, AND friends who do not have LD. Like Kenny, you can have both kinds of friends!

What is the best way to make and keep friends? Be a friendly person. Here are some tips to help you be a friendly person.

10 Tips for Making and Keeping Friends

1. Watch other kids in class and on the playground. See if you can find some who play without teasing or fighting. They would probably make good friends.

2. Take part in games on the playground where kids line up to take turns.

3. Watch to see what other kids like. Find out as much as you can about what they like. Then you can talk with them about the things they like.

4. Do not try to *make* other kids be your friends, especially the most popular ones. You might find good friends in students who are not part of the "in crowd." Is there someone who seems shy? Maybe that person is waiting for you to act friendly first.

5. Do not wander around the playground by yourself and hope someone will ask you to play. Instead, choose a game and ask someone to join you.

6. When you play with others, say nice things to them, take your turn, and be a good sport.

7. Do not show off or get into trouble to get noticed.

8. Most people like to talk about themselves. Ask other kids questions about what they like to do. Or ask them about their favorite TV shows, sports, or games.

9. Be friendly, share things, and do not tease. Treat other kids the way you want them to treat you. (That is right: This is the Golden Rule!)

10. Like yourself. Kids like other kids who like themselves.

Chapter 11

Eight Ways to Get Along at Home

By now you know that you are not stupid. You know you are doing your best work. But maybe other people, like your parents, do not know you are doing your best work.

Maybe your parents have told you, "We know you can do as well as other kids IF YOU WORK HARD." Maybe they are not the only ones who think this. Sometimes teachers will say things like this to parents of kids with LD:

⭐ "Your child would do fine if he was not so lazy."

⭐ "Your child is smart enough. She just does not pay attention in class."

⭐ "Your child could do good work if he cared more and acted up less."

Then parents tell the kids, "You are lazy." Or, "You do not pay attention in class." Or, "You do not care about school. You act up too much."

When this happens, kids get upset. If it happens to you, *you* probably get upset. No matter how hard you try in school, you still have a hard time at home!

Maybe it starts right after school. As soon as you get home, your mom or dad greets you at the door. They want you to do your homework RIGHT NOW! It seems like they *never* let up on you.

Summers are not any better. Most kids get to do what they want all summer. They do not even have to think about school for THREE WHOLE MONTHS. Not you, though. You have to go to summer school!

Read what these kids say about their parents:

"Mom cares about me. She tries to help. My dad doesn't understand my problems. It makes me nervous. He thinks I can really hear." —Jesse, 11

"My mom and dad feel good that I'm learning, but they want me to learn better. Sometimes they get mad at me when I don't understand what they want." —John, 11

"I am myself around my parents, and if they're mad I listen to them usually, but sometimes I just ignore them." —Stacy, 12

Why do your parents push you to do better all the time? They know you are not stupid. They want you to be the best you can be. They think that if you work harder, you will do better.

Parents do not always understand that kids DO work hard at school. They do not know that kids need time to RELAX.

Maybe you and your parents get upset with each other. They yell at you. You yell back. What follows is one big fight.

But fighting does not help. Talking is better. And talking about your feelings is best. Tell your parents how you feel and how hard you work at school. Tell them you do not want to have a hard time at home.

Easy to say, right? Not so easy to do. It is hard to talk out loud about your feelings. Many kids with LD have the same problems with their parents.

Here are some ideas to share with your parents. They are all ways to make things better at home. If you just cannot talk to your parents, maybe you can show them these ideas.

1. Tell your parents you need time to relax.

Most parents go to work. When they come home from work, do they keep doing that same work? No. To work at the same job 16 hours a day is not fun.

Going to school is your work. If you have to do homework all night, too, that is like working all the time.

This does not mean that you should never do homework. It means that you should also have time to relax. And you should do more relaxing at home than working.

2. Tell your parents if your homework takes too long.

Homework may be good practice for you. And your parents probably think homework is important. Maybe they make sure you do your homework every night.

But do you feel that you are spending ALL of your time doing homework with NO time left over? Then your homework takes too long. To find out why, ask yourself these questions:

★ Is it hard to understand what you are supposed to do?

★ Is it hard for you to write neatly?

★ Is it hard to keep the numbers lined up for math?

★ Are you tired from doing schoolwork all day?

Did you answer YES to any of these questions? Then tell your parents or teachers. Or ask your parents to talk to your teachers. Your parents should tell them how long it takes for you to do your homework.

You need time for yourself, too. Ask your parents and teachers if you can work out a plan. The plan should let you do homework and still have time left just for you.

3. Tell your parents good news about you.

Sometimes parents are asked to come to school to hear about problems. Maybe their children are not doing their schoolwork. Maybe they are acting up. Maybe they are talking back to the teacher.

It is hard for parents to hear bad news. Some parents hear a lot more bad news than good news.

Tell your parents good news about you. Tell them the things you do right each day. Tell them when you are getting better at your schoolwork. Or when the teacher says something nice to you. Or when you make a new friend.

What if your parents are asked to come to school? They can hear good things about you, not just problems. They can tell the people at the school good things about you. Maybe your teachers think you are lazy or not trying. Maybe they do not understand you. Your parents can help. They can tell your teachers what you are really like.

4. Take time out when you need it.

Sometimes you may feel so upset that you just want to scream or run away and hide.

When you feel that way, take time out. Go for a walk. Go to your room, close the door, and listen to music. Ride your bike. Go fishing.

Do something you like to do. Do NOT do schoolwork.

5. Make a plan for your time.

One way to get things done is to make a list or a plan for your time.

Do you have trouble remembering what school-work you should do at home? Make a list of the things you are supposed to do at home. Write on your list everything you need to bring home. Bring the list home, too. Make a check by each thing on your list after you do it.

Decide what time you will do your schoolwork. Right after you get home? After dinner? Pick a time when someone is there to help you if you need help.

Before you start your homework, find everything you need. Pencils, books, papers? What else? Turn off the TV and the radio. Do not call up friends on the telephone or start emailing them on the computer. Perhaps you can even put a DO NOT DISTURB sign on your table. Then WORK!

6. Eat well.

Did you know that "junk foods" like soda, chips, and candy make it harder to think? Healthy foods like fruits and vegetables can help you think better.

If you need a snack, eat the good stuff. Skip the junk food. Do your brain a favor!

7. Get a job.

Get a paper route, baby-sit, or cut the neighbor's lawn. Collect and sell cans.

Getting a job will help keep your mind off of school. It will help you think about what you want to do when you get out of school. You will also make some money.

On page 87 of this book, there is a part called, "A Few Words About Home and Homework." Show this part to your parents. It can help them to understand why you need time away from school.

8. Find a hobby.

Find something you like to do that gets your mind off school. Keep a pet. Collect rocks. Exercise. Listen to music. Learn to use a computer.

Finding a hobby will also give you something to share with others. You may even become an expert.

Remember that being an expert is a good way to show that people with LD can be smart. It is also a good way to get attention.

Chapter 12

Tips to Remember as You Grow Up

Right now you might think, "I will *never* get out of school!" But you will be out of school and grown-up before you know it. Maybe you think that once you are out of school, all your problems will be over. No more teachers on your back. No more nagging from your parents. You will be on your own. You can do what you want!

This is not the way it is. Being an adult is not easy. Doing just what you want can get you into trouble. When you become an adult, you must take care of yourself. Many of the things that help you in school right now will also help you as you become an adult. As you go through middle school and high school, and as you become an adult, it will be helpful to remember the following points.

Ask for help. You are learning how to do many things for yourself. But some things you will need help with. Do not be afraid to ask for help. You can ask your teachers, parents, friends, relatives, or other adults you trust.

Get organized. Many kids with LD learn better when they are organized. School is easier and more fun when they remember to do their homework and bring the right materials to class. Ask your parents or teachers for help if you feel like you are not organized. They can teach you how to use an assignment book or how to make "to-do" lists.

Have a good work ethic. Even if some things are hard for you, you should always keep trying to do your best and not give up. Tell yourself you are going to spend so much time every day working on your homework or a project. As it was said earlier, never use your LD as an excuse for not doing your work. Always work hard and be proud of your efforts!

Have a positive attitude. You will have good days and bad days. Everybody does! It is important to not get down on yourself. People like to be around others who are upbeat and positive. There are many things you are good at. Remember that you can learn, you just learn some things differently. Have confidence in yourself and tell yourself "I can do it!"

Stay out of trouble. School is not much fun if you are in trouble all of the time. You can learn to stay out of trouble. You can learn to stay away from kids who are up to no good or who are always fighting or teasing other kids. You can make positive choices.

Set goals. It is easier to be successful when you know what you are working toward. Make a plan for what goals you want to reach. Decide what steps you need to take to help you reach your goals. Work hard and believe in yourself!

A Happy Ending: You Can Be a Winner!

We would like to tell you about two people, Anita and Trever, who are adults who have LD.

Anita has finished six years of college. Now she is a school counselor. She still has a hard time with spelling, and she reads slowly.

All through school, Anita had to study very hard. But she is very bright. She is also a very friendly person. Anita is a person with LD, and she is a winner.

Trever went to LD classes all through high school. He finished high school, but he did not want to go to college. He wanted to fix cars.

Trever got a job as a helper at a car repair shop. He always went to work on time, worked hard, and was polite. Trever also tried to learn everything he could about fixing cars. He asked questions and watched carefully.

Soon Trever got promoted to car mechanic. He did so well that he was made the supervisor of the shop. He still has a hard time reading and must ask for help sometimes. Trever is a person with LD, and he is a winner.

You can be a winner, too. There is no magic cure for LD. There is no pill, way of teaching, or diet that can make you not have LD. But having LD does not stop a person from doing great things and being happy and successful.

Now that you have read this book, you know there are ways to make things better at school and at home. Use these suggestions and remember:

You are a person with LD.

You are also a great kid.

You are a WINNER!

Ten More Things You Might Want to Know About LD

When kids find out they have LD, they want to know more about it. Here are 10 questions kids ask about LD.

If your parents and teachers want to know more about LD, you can show them these pages.

1. Is dyslexia the same thing as LD?

Dyslexia is a kind of LD in which a person has trouble reading words, sentences, or paragraphs. But not all people with reading problems have dyslexia.

Studies show that people with dyslexia use a different part of the brain than people who do not have dyslexia. A person with dyslexia may show some of the following problems:

★ reads very slowly and makes many mistakes

★ has trouble spelling; many times will spell the same word differently in the same assignment

★ may have trouble answering open-ended questions on tests

★ may have a hard time learning a foreign language

★ may have poor memory skills

★ misreads information

★ may have trouble planning, organizing, and managing time, materials, and tasks

★ has a hard time with the order of letters in words

★ may have trouble rhyming words

★ may have a hard time pronouncing words (may reverse sounds)

Only about one to three percent of people with reading problems have dyslexia. The others cannot read well because of other problems. These problems might be:

★ they have trouble sitting still

★ they do not have enough interest in reading

★ they are not paying attention

Some people with LD can read well, but they have trouble in other areas such as math, language (talking and listening), or making friends.

2. Does having LD mean that I have brain damage?

That is a good question. Even the experts have trouble answering it.

About 100 years ago, some doctors saw that some smart kids had trouble learning. Those kids were like people who had strokes, a disease that causes brain damage. Both kinds of people can have problems with language (talking and listening), planning things, and moving their bodies.

Years later, some other doctors saw that kids with LD were like soldiers with head injuries. Both kinds of people had many of the same problems, like problems with language (talking and listening). So, many doctors today do think that kids with LD may have brain damage.

But other doctors do not agree. They think kids with LD have problems because they started school too early. Or they did not get enough help, or the right kind of help, from parents or teachers.

Perhaps a few kids with LD do have brain damage. But no one knows for sure.

3. Does LD ever go away?

This is a hard question. The answer depends on many things, like:

★ How many ways does the person have LD? Only in one way, like reading? Or in many ways?

★ How early did parents and teachers find out about the LD? Since then, what kind of help has the person with LD been given?

★ How helpful has the person's school been? Do the teachers, principal, and psychologist know about LD? Have they tried to learn more about it and understand it better?

★ How helpful have the person's parents been? How much do they know about LD?

★ How independent has the person with LD
been allowed to be?

And if the person with LD is an adult:

★ What kind of work does the person with LD
do? Has this person had good work experiences? Did he or she have help finding and
choosing a job after school was over?

While LD may not go away, most people with LD
can do many things if they have the right help. This
help must begin very early in their lives.

4. Can I go to college if I have LD?

This is a hard question, too. It depends on what kind
of help you get, and how hard it is for you to do
schoolwork. It depends on how much you want to go
to college, and how important college is to get the job
you want.

You need to finish college to get only about nine
percent of the jobs in this country. Some people with
LD do finish college. Many others have a hard time
with it and never finish.

We do not think that going to college is something you have to do. Going to college does not mean
that a person will be happy and successful as an adult.
But if you want to go to college, you should try. Ask
your parents and teachers what they think. Ask them
to help you try.

Think about what kind of college you might want
to go to. There are four-year colleges, two-year
colleges, and junior colleges.

There are colleges you can go to in the evenings so
you can have a job at the same time. These schools

are not as big or confusing as the four-year colleges, and you could take other kinds of classes at the same time. When you finish there, you can decide if you want to go to college some more.

If you decide to go to a four-year college, choose one that has special programs for people with LD. Many colleges do. For help in finding these colleges, contact the following organizations and ask them to send you information about colleges for people with LD:

American Council on Education
One Dupont Circle NW
Washington, DC 20036
(202) 939-9300
www.acenet.edu

Learning Disabilities Association of America (LDA)
4156 Library Road
Pittsburgh, PA 15234
(412) 341-1515
www.ldanatl.org

National Center for Learning Disabilities (NCLD)
381 Park Avenue South, Suite 1401
New York, NY 10016
1-888-575-7373
www.ncld.org

Here is a book that you can check out from the library:

Peterson's Colleges with Programs for Students with Learning Disabilities or Attention Deficit Disorders, edited by Charles T. Mangrum II, Ed.D., and Stephen S. Strichart, Ph.D. (Princeton, NJ: Peterson's Guides, 2000).

If you do not want to go to college you can make other plans. Go to vocational school. Become a graphic designer, a hair stylist, a mechanic, an animal-doctor's helper, or a computer repair-person. Try to think about what you are good at. Then get some training in that area.

Here are some books that can help you make plans without college:

Unlocking Potential: College and Other Choices for People with LD and ADHD edited by Juliana M. Taymans, Ph.D., and Lynda L. West, Ph.D., with Madeline Sullivan, M.A. (Bathesda, MD: Woodbine House, 2000).

Success Without a College Degree: Dissolving the Roadblocks Between You and Success by John T. Murphy (Seattle, WA: Achievement Dynamics, Inc., 2001).

5. If I have children, will they have LD?

No one knows for sure. It is true that some families have many people with LD. Not just brothers and sisters, but cousins and nieces and uncles as well.

We do not know why these families have many people with LD. Did they inherit it? Or did they get it because they have the same background and many of the same experiences?

Inherit (in HER it)

means "to get it from your parents or grandparents."

If you decide to have children of your own, talk to a doctor or an LD teacher. They can tell you more about your chances of having kids with LD.

Many people with LD have children who do have LD. Many people with LD have children who do not have LD. Here is what you need to think about: Could you love and take care of a child, no matter what? That is the most important thing to decide.

6. Will I be able to work and live on my own someday?

Most people with LD can become as independent as other people. It just may take more planning and work. That is why we think you should start to prepare for your future right now.

Start thinking about all you will need to do to be a good worker and live on your own. Get practice by working as soon as you can. You can get a paper route, work on a ranch, or get a job in a fast-food restaurant.

The earlier you learn about work, the more likely you will learn the skills you need to be a good worker.

We also think it is important for you to learn to make your own decisions. Practice being independent as soon as you can. Make choices about the clothes you wear. Finish your schoolwork on your own. Help with work around the house. There are many things you can do!

7. Do all kids with LD read and write words backwards?

No. Very few kids with LD have this problem. It is called "mirror writing." Everything they see looks the way it would look in a mirror.

Many young children ages seven and eight see letters and words backwards when they are first learning to read and write. This is not a problem unless it keeps up as the children grow older.

If you have this problem, visit a psychologist who works with people with LD. Ask your school psychologist, counselor, or social worker for the names of some psychologists. Then tell your parents the names.

8. Are all kids with LD alike?

NO! Kids with LD can be very different from each other. (Just like other kids.) But there is one way they are alike: It is hard for them to learn. That is why they are in the same LD classes at school.

9. Are there more boys or girls with LD?

Three out of every four kids with LD are boys. No one knows why. Maybe boys are more likely to inherit LD (get it from their parents or grandparents). We do know that more boys inherit health problems than girls do.

Also, boys are more active than girls. Sometimes it is harder for them to sit still in school. They may act up more and seem less interested in doing schoolwork. Teachers and parents might think they have LD when they really do not.

10. Should all kids with LD be put in regular classes?

No. IDEA (Individuals with Disabilities Education Act) says that kids should be taught in the right kind of classes to help them learn. Some kids with LD do fine in a regular classroom. Others learn best in an LD classroom.

LD classes are often better for learning. They are smaller, quieter, and less confusing. Plus the LD teacher knows how to teach in ways that will help LD kids learn.

Resources

Recommended Resources for Parents and Teachers

Adelizzi, J., and Goss, D. *Parenting Children with Learning Disabilities.* Westport, CT: Bergin & Garvey, 2001.

Armstrong, T. *The Myth of the A.D.D. Child: 50 Ways to Improve Your Child's Behavior and Attention Span Without Drugs, Labels, or Coercion.* New York: Plume, 1997.

Citro, T. *The Experts Speak: Parenting the Child with Learning Disabilities.* Waltham, MA: LDMA, 1998.

Cunningham, P., and Allington, R. *Classrooms That Work: They Can All Read and Write.* Boston, MA: Allyn & Bacon, 2010.

Faber, A., and Mazlish, E. *How to Talk So Kids Can Learn: At Home and In School.* New York: Fireside, 1996.

Flick, G. L. *ADD/ADHD Behavior-Change Resource Kit: Ready-to-Use Strategies & Activities for Helping Children with Attention Deficit Disorder.* West Nyack, NY: The Center for Applied Research in Education, 1998.

Freed, J., and Parsons, L. *Right-Brained Children in a Left-Brained World: Unlocking the Potential of Your ADD Child.* New York: Fireside, 1998.

Greenbaum, J., & Markel, G. *Helping Adolescents with ADHD & Learning Disabilities: Ready-to-Use Tips, Techniques, and Checklists for School Success.* Hoboken, NJ: Jossey-Bass, 2001.

Harwell, J. *Complete Learning Disabilities Handbook: Ready-to-Use Strategies and Activities for Teaching Students with Learning Disabilities.* Hoboken, NJ: Jossey-Bass, 2008.

Heacox, D. *Differentiating Instruction in the Regular Classroom: How to Reach and Teach All Learners, Grades 3–12.* Minneapolis: Free Spirit Publishing, 2008.

Levine, M. *A Mind at a Time.* New York: Simon & Schuster, 2002.

Markel, G., & Greenbaum, J. *Performance Breakthroughs for Adolescents with Learning Disabilities or ADD: How to Help Students Succeed in the Regular Education Classroom.* Champaign, IL: Research Press, 2000.

Rief, S. F. *How to Reach and Teach ADD/ADHD Children: Practical Techniques, Strategies, and Interventions for Helping Children with Attention Problems and Hyperactivity.* Hoboken, NJ: Jossey-Bass, 1993.

Rimm, S. *Smart Parenting: How to Raise a Happy, Achieving Child.* New York: Crown Publishers, 1996.

Schumm, J. S. *How to Help Your Child with Homework: The Complete Guide to Encouraging Good Study Habits and Ending the Homework Wars.* Minneapolis: Free Spirit Publishing, 2005.

Silver, L. *The Misunderstood Child: Understanding and Coping with Your Child's Learning Disabilities.* New York: Three Rivers Press, 2006.

Vail, P. L. *Smart Kids with School Problems: Things to Know and Ways to Help.* New York: Dutton, 1989.

Winebrenner, S. *Teaching Kids with Learning Difficulties in the Regular Classroom: Ways to Challenge & Motivate Struggling Students to Achieve Proficiency with Required Standards.* Minneapolis: Free Spirit Publishing, 2006.

Recommended Books for Improving School Skills

Hayes, M. *The Tuned-In, Turned-On Book About Learning Problems.* Novato, CA: Academic Therapy Publications, 1994.

Levine, M. *Keeping a Head in School: A Student's Book About Learning Abilities and Learning Disorders.* Cambridge, MA: Educators Publishing Service, 1991.

Quinn, P. O., and Stern, J. M. *The "Putting on the Brakes" Activity Book for Young People with ADHD.* Washington, DC: Magination Press, 1993.

Quinn, P. O., and Stern, J. M., editors. *The Best of "Brakes": An Activity Book for Kids with ADD and ADHD.* Washington, DC: Magination Press, 2000.

Schumm, J. S. *School Power: Study Skill Strategies for Succeeding in School (Revised and Updated Edition).* Minneapolis: Free Spirit Publishing, 2001.

A Few Words About Home and Homework

All of us who are parents want to be good parents. We think that one way to do this is to make sure our kids do their homework. There is nothing wrong with this way of thinking, at least where most kids are concerned. However, if your child has learning differences, you might want to be careful not to pressure your child too much about homework.

For most kids with LD, school is tough. It is tough all day, every day. Try to imagine what it is like to be frustrated all day long, and then come home and be forced to do *more* school-work until bedtime.

We believe that home should be a haven for children with learning differences. Home should be a place where they can relax and be themselves. If you feel that your child's teachers are assigning too much homework, try asking them to consider assigning less homework. Why assign 50 math problems if the student can work 5–10 correctly? An assignment that takes most other kids 15 minutes to complete might take a child with learning differences at least an hour to finish.

Recommended Books for Promoting Self-Awareness and Self-Esteem

Abeel, S. *Reach for the Moon*. Duluth, MN: Pfeiffer-Hamilton Publishers, 1994.

Armstrong, T. *You're Smarter Than You Think: A Kid's Guide to Multiple Intelligences*. Minneapolis: Free Spirit Publishing, 2002.

Canfield, J. and Wells, H. C. *100 Ways to Enhance Self-Concept in the Classroom*. Boston, MA: Allyn & Bacon, 1994.

Dwyer, K. *What Do You Mean, I Have a Learning Disability?* New York: Walker and Company, 1991.

Flynn, M. C., and Flynn, P. *Having a Learning Disability*. Mankato, MN: Smart Apple Media, 1999.

Gehret, J. *The Don't-Give-Up Kid and Learning Differences*. Fairport, NY: Verbal Images Press, 2009.

Gordon, M. *Jumpin' Johnny Get Back to Work! A Child's Guide to ADHD/Hyperactivity*. DeWitt, NY: GSI Publications, 1991.

Gordon, M. *My Brother's a World-Class Pain: A Sibling's Guide to ADHD/Hyperactivity*. DeWitt, NY: GSI Publications, 1992.

Kaufman, G., et. al. *Stick Up for Yourself! Every Kid's Guide to Personal Power and Positive Self-Esteem (Revised and Updated)*. Minneapolis: Free Spirit Publishing, 1999.

Levine, M. D. *All Kinds of Minds: A Young Student's Book About Learning Abilities and Learning Disorders.* Cambridge, MA: Educators Publishing Service, 1992.

Nadeau, K. G., and Dixon, E. B. *Learning to Slow Down and Pay Attention: A Book for Kids About ADHD.* Washington, DC: Magination Press, 2004.

Quinn, P. O., and Stern, J. M. *Putting on the Brakes: Young People's Guide to Understanding Attention Deficit Hyperactivity Disorder (ADHD).* Washington, DC: Magination Press, 2001.

A Few Words About Depression

Children who are depressed may exhibit a wide variety of symptoms, making diagnosis difficult. Like depressed adults, children may cry easily and frequently, have sleeping and eating problems, and be tired or sick a great deal. Unlike adults, depressed children are sometimes sullen, hostile, and aggressive. They may throw tantrums over small issues or strike out at others in reaction to seemingly insignificant events.

Kids with LD are more likely to become depressed than other children due to their difficulty in understanding their condition and the frustrations they encounter. In most schools, a school counselor, psychologist, or social worker will be available to guide you to

(continued)

the most appropriate places to receive assistance if you believe that your child is depressed. In some communities, you may need to contact a community mental health center or your family physician for diagnostic assistance and referrals.

Books that promote a positive self-concept and assist children in self-understanding may facilitate a child's expression of his or her feelings. The books listed on pages 88–89 are especially appropriate for young people with LD, their parents, and teachers. Parents, we recommend that you consult with your child's teacher and school counselor before choosing any materials to try at home. Teachers, please talk to the parents, as well as the school counselor, psychologist, or social worker.

Educational Software/ Multimedia Companies

ABLEDATA
8630 Fenton Street, Suite 930
Silver Spring, MD 20910
1-800-227-0216
www.abledata.com

A.D.D. WareHouse
300 Northwest 70th Avenue, Suite 102
Plantation, FL 33317
1-800-233-9273
www.addwarehouse.com

Attainment Company, Inc.
504 Commerce Parkway
P.O. Box 930160
Verona, WI 53593-0160
1-800-327-4269
www.attainmentcompany.com

CompassLearning, Inc.
203 Colorado Street
Austin, TX 78701
1-800-232-9556
www.compasslearning.com

Franklin Electronic Publishers
One Franklin Plaza
Burlington, NJ 08016-4907
1-800-266-5626
www.franklin.com

Heartsoft Educational Software
Heartsoft, LLC
8252 South Harvard Avenue, Suite 100
Tulsa, OK 74137
1-800-285-3475
www.heartsoft.com

Learning Seed
641 West Lake Street, Suite 301
Chicago, IL 60661
1-800-634-4941
www.learningseed.com

Marsh Media
P.O. Box 8082
Shawnee Mission, KS 66208
1-800-821-3303
www.marshmedia.com

Scholastic Inc.
557 Broadway
New York, NY 10012
1-800-724-6527
www.scholastic.com

Sunburst Technology
1550 Executive Drive
Elgin, IL 60123
1-800-321-7511
www.sunburst.com

Organizations

Attention Deficit Disorder Association (ADDA)
P.O. Box 7557
Wilmington, DE 19803
1-800-939-1019
www.add.org
ADDA aims to help people with ADHD lead happier, more successful lives through education, research, and public advocacy. Their Web site offers articles, personal stories, interviews with ADHD professionals, book reviews, and links to other ADHD-related sites.

Children and Adults with Attention Deficit/Hyperactivity Disorder (CHADD)
8181 Professional Place, Suite 150
Landover, MD 20785
1-800-233-4050
www.chadd.org
CHADD is the nation's largest nonprofit organization serving individuals with ADHD, providing resources, support, and advocacy efforts.

The Council for Exceptional Children (CEC)
1110 North Glebe Road, Suite 300
Arlington, VA 22201
1-888-232-7733
www.cec.sped.org
CEC is a professional organization dedicated to improving the quality of education for *all* exceptional children. Their online journal *(CEC Today)* keeps professionals abreast of research and CEC's efforts toward improving work conditions.

The International Dyslexia Association (IDA)
40 York Road, 4th Floor
Baltimore, MD 21204
(410) 296-0232
www.interdys.org
IDA is a nonprofit organization dedicated to helping individuals with dyslexia, their families, and the communities that support them.

Learning Disabilities Association of America (LDA)
4156 Library Road
Pittsburgh, PA 15234
(412) 341-1515
www.ldanatl.org
Members of LDA include professionals and parents
devoted to advancing the education and well-being
of children and adults with learning differences.
Visit their Web site for information on state and
local chapters.

National Center for Learning Disabilities (NCLD)
381 Park Avenue South, Suite 1401
New York, NY 10016
1-888-575-7373
www.ncld.org
NCLD provides national leadership in support of
children and adults with learning disabilities. They
offer referral services, develop and advocate for educational programs, and promote public awareness.

**National Dissemination Center for Children with
Disabilities (NICHCY)**
1825 Connecticut Avenue NW, Suite 700
Washington, DC 20009
1-800-695-0285
www.nichcy.org
NICHCY is a national information and referral center
that provides information on disabilities to families,
educators, and other professionals. A wide variety of
publications are available at their Web site, including
fact sheets on specific disabilities, state resource
sheets, parent guides, bibliographies, and more.

Web Sites

ERIC Clearinghouse on Disabilities and Gifted Education (ERICEC)

eric.hoagiesgifted.org

ERIC provides information on the education of individuals with disabilities as well as those who are gifted. The network contains digests, fact sheets, FAQs, and links to other online resources.

HEATH Resource Center

www.heath.gwu.edu

Operated by George Washington University, HEATH is a national clearinghouse on postsecondary educa tion for individuals with disabilities. In partnership with the U.S. Department of Education, it provides information about support services, policies, procedures, adaptations, and opportunities at institutions of higher education.

IDEA 2004

idea.ed.gov

This site is designed to answer questions about the Individuals with Disabilities Education Act and works in partnership with service providers, administrators, families and advocates, and policymakers to support efforts to help all children learn and progress.

LD OnLine
www.ldonline.org
This Web site about learning disabilities is for parents, teachers, and other professionals. It provides the latest news and research, offers LD materials and information, and includes the monthly column by leading LD expert, Richard Lavoie, entitled "Tales from the Road."

Wrightslaw
www.wrightslaw.com
This site provides parents, advocates, educators, and attorneys accurate, up-to-date information, articles, cases, newsletters, and resources about special education law and advocacy for children with disabilities.

Index

Meet the Authors

Hi! I'm Gary Fisher. I went to college for many years to study LD, and I have written about LD. Most importantly, I worked with over 1,000 kids with LD in the ten years I spent as a school psychologist in Washington State. Today, I live in Las Vegas, Nevada, and I am a professor in the College of Health and Human Sciences at the University of Nevada, Reno. I have three children, Colin, Brooke, and Aaron.

Hello! My name is Rhoda Cummings. I studied special education in college. Now I live in Reno, Nevada, and I am a professor of Educational Psychology at the University of Nevada, Reno. I have two children, Carter and Courtney. My son, Carter, has LD. He has his own apartment, drives his own car, and has a full-time job.

Gary and Rhoda are also the authors of *The Survival Guide for Teenagers with LD; When Your Child Has LD: A Survival Guide for Parents;* and *The School Survival Guide for Kids with LD;* which are now out of print but may be found in libraries.